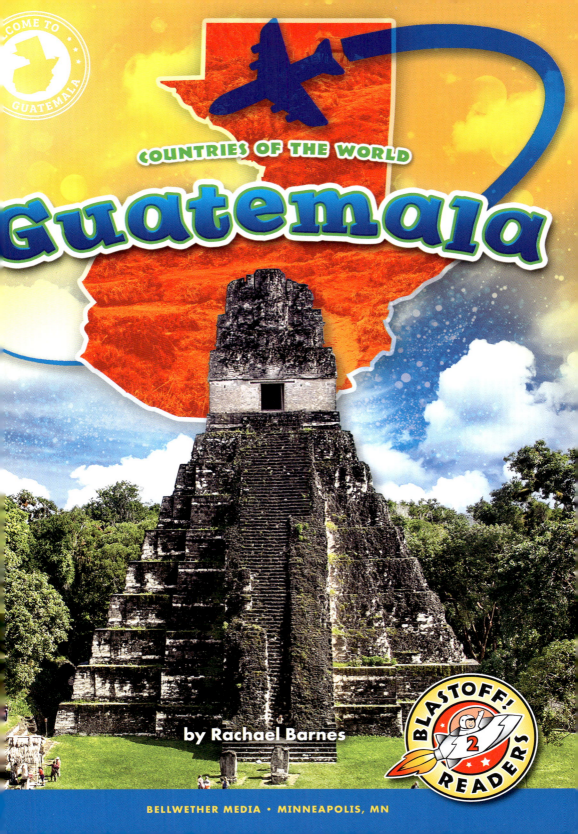

Blastoff! Readers are carefully developed by literacy experts to build reading stamina and move students toward fluency by combining standards-based content with developmentally appropriate text.

Level 1 provides the most support through repetition of high-frequency words, light text, predictable sentence patterns, and strong visual support.

Level 2 offers early readers a bit more challenge through varied sentences, increased text load, and text-supportive special features.

Level 3 advances early-fluent readers toward fluency through increased text load, less reliance on photos, advancing concepts, longer sentences, and more complex special features.

★ **Blastoff! Universe**

Reading Level

Grade K

Grades 1–3

Grade 4

This edition first published in 2023 by Bellwether Media, Inc.

No part of this publication may be reproduced in whole or in part without written permission of the publisher. For information regarding permission, write to Bellwether Media, Inc., Attention: Permissions Department, 6012 Blue Circle Drive, Minnetonka, MN 55343.

Library of Congress Cataloging-in-Publication Data

Names: Barnes, Rachael, author.
Title: Guatemala / by Rachael Barnes.
Description: Minneapolis, MN : Bellwether Media, 2023. | Series: Blastoff! Readers: Countries of the world | Includes bibliographical references and index. | Audience: Ages 5-8 | Audience: Grades 2-3 | Summary: "Relevant images match informative text in this introduction to Guatemala. Intended for students in kindergarten through third grade"— Provided by publisher.
Identifiers: LCCN 2022044252 (print) | LCCN 2022044253 (ebook) | ISBN 9798886871319 (library binding) | ISBN 9798886872576 (ebook)
Subjects: LCSH: Guatemala–Juvenile literature.
Classification: LCC F1463.2 .B376 2023 (print) | LCC F1463.2 (ebook) | DDC 972.81–dc23/eng/20220913
LC record available at https://lccn.loc.gov/2022044252
LC ebook record available at https://lccn.loc.gov/2022044253

Text copyright © 2023 by Bellwether Media, Inc. BLASTOFF! READERS and associated logos are trademarks and/or registered trademarks of Bellwether Media, Inc.

Editor: Elizabeth Neuenfeldt   Designer: Gabriel Hilger

Printed in the United States of America, North Mankato, MN.

Table of Contents

All About Guatemala	4
Land and Animals	6
Life in Guatemala	12
Guatemala Facts	20
Glossary	22
To Learn More	23
Index	24

All About Guatemala

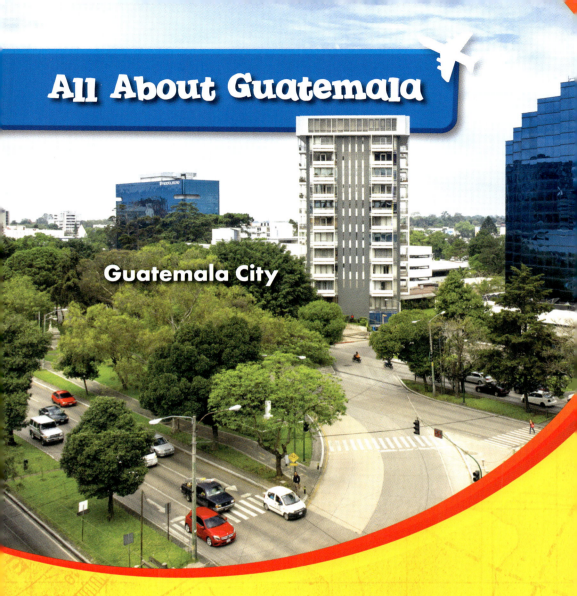

Guatemala City

Guatemala is a country in **Central America**. It touches the Pacific Ocean and the Caribbean Sea.

Guatemala City is the capital. It is the biggest city in Central America!

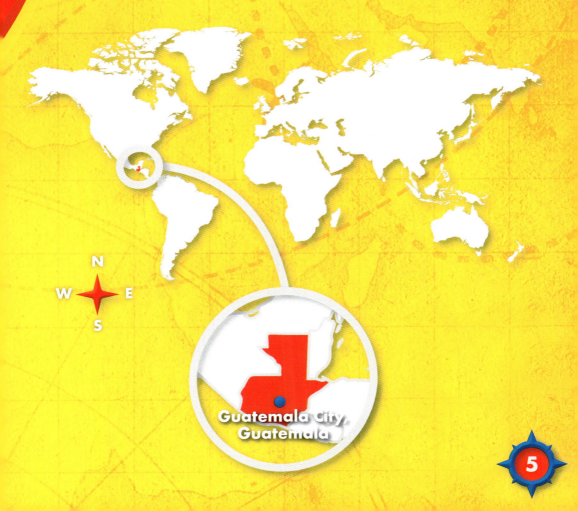

Land and Animals

Mountains rise over much of Guatemala. Some of them are **volcanoes**! Tajumulco Volcano is the tallest.

Rain forests cover the north. Beaches line the west coast.

rain forest

Tajumulco Volcano

Size: 13,845 feet (4,220 meters) tall
Famous For:
the tallest point in Central America

Guatemala's weather is mostly **tropical**.

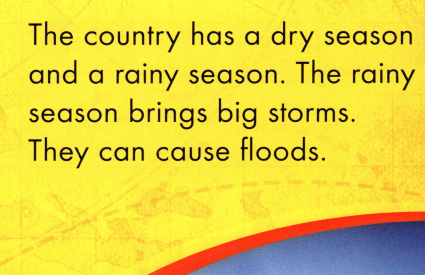

The country has a dry season and a rainy season. The rainy season brings big storms. They can cause floods.

flood

Quetzals fly in the mountains. Howler monkeys call loudly in the rain forests. Jaguars hunt nearby.

quetzal

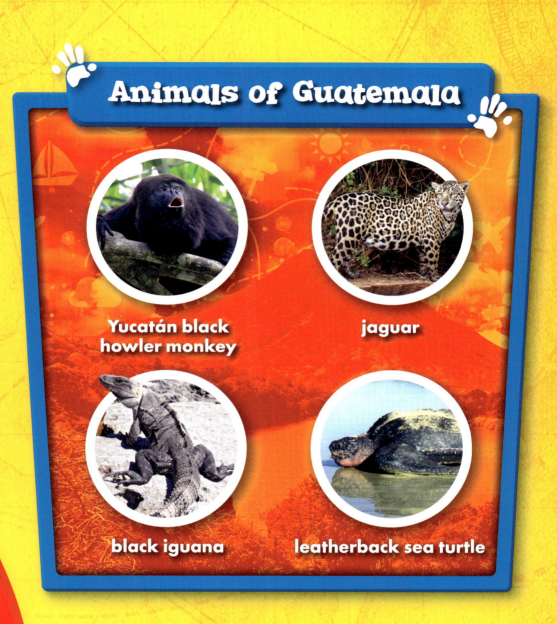

Animals of Guatemala

Yucatán black howler monkey

jaguar

black iguana

leatherback sea turtle

Black iguanas rest on warm rocks. Sea turtles swim along the west coast.

Life in Guatemala

About half of all Guatemalans live in cities. **Indigenous** peoples often live in the countryside.

Many Guatemalans are **Catholic**. Spanish is widely spoken.

Catholic church

Soccer is a favorite sport. Guatemalan teams play around the world.

Families visit the beach.
Some enjoy the traveling circus!
Marimba music is popular
throughout the country.

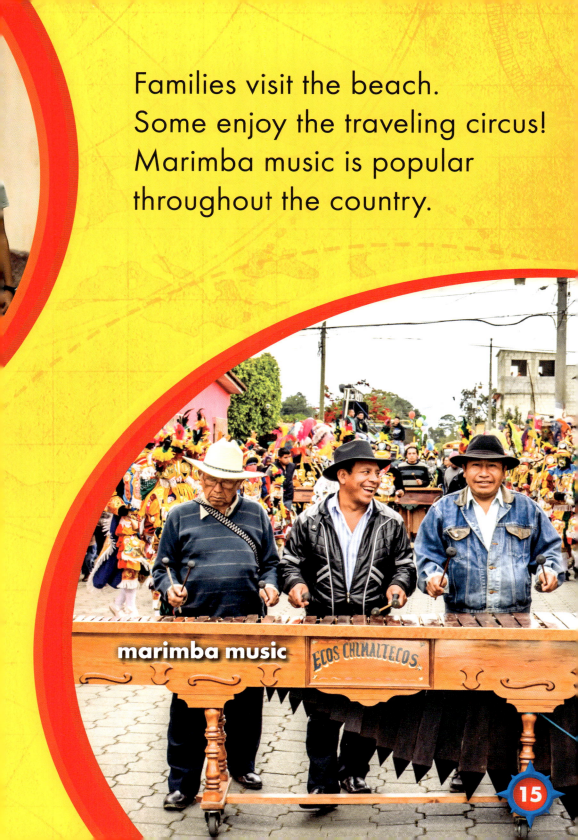

marimba music

Pepián is a favorite stew. It has vegetables and meat. Rice and corn are **staples**.

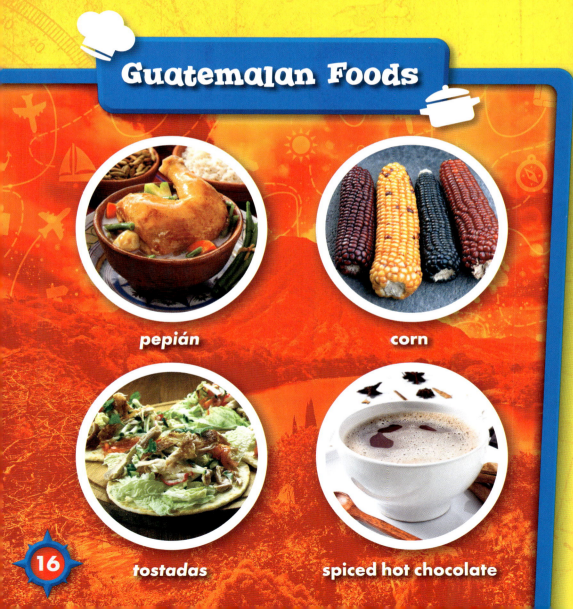

Guatemalan Foods

pepián

corn

tostadas

spiced hot chocolate

Tostadas are a common snack. Spiced hot chocolate is a sweet dessert!

Semana Santa

Semana Santa is the week of Easter. People enjoy colorful parades.

Rab'in Ajaw is a summer **festival**. It honors Indigenous **traditions**. People dance and tell stories. Holidays bring Guatemalans together!

Guatemala Facts

Size:
42,042 square miles
(108,889 square kilometers)

Population:
17,703,190 (2022)

National Holiday:
Independence Day (September 15)

Main Language:
Spanish

Capital City:
Guatemala City

Famous Face

Name: Gaby Moreno

Famous For: award-winning singer, songwriter, and music producer whose music has been on several popular TV shows

Religions

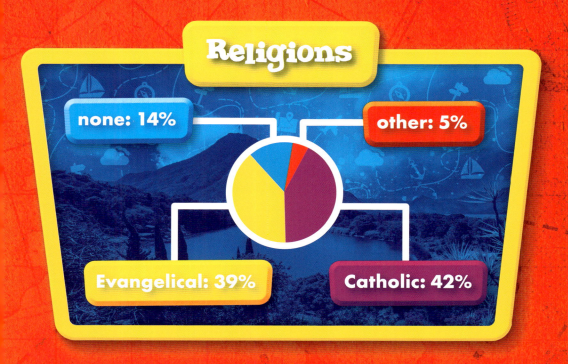

- none: 14%
- other: 5%
- Evangelical: 39%
- Catholic: 42%

Top Landmarks

Antigua

Lake Atitlán

Tikal National Park

Glossary

Catholic—relating to the Christian church that is led by the pope

Central America—the narrow, southern part of North America; this region includes Belize, Costa Rica, El Salvador, Guatemala, Honduras, Nicaragua, and Panama.

festival—a time or event of celebration

Indigenous—related to people originally from an area

rain forests—thick, green forests that receive a lot of rain

staples—widely used foods or other items

traditions—customs, ideas, or beliefs handed down from one generation to the next

tropical—relating to a warm place near the equator; the equator is the imaginary line that divides Earth into northern and southern halves.

volcanoes—holes in the earth; when a volcano erupts, hot ash, gas, or melted rock called lava shoots out.

To Learn More

AT THE LIBRARY

Davies, Monika. *Mexico*. Minneapolis, Minn.: Bellwether Media, 2023.

Esbaum, Jill. *Sea Turtles*. Washington, D.C.: National Geographic Kids, 2021.

Mattern, Joanne. *Guatemala*. Egremont, Mass.: Red Chair Press, 2019.

ON THE WEB

Factsurfer.com gives you a safe, fun way to find more information.

1. Go to www.factsurfer.com.

2. Enter "Guatemala" into the search box and click 🔍.

3. Select your book cover to see a list of related content.

Index

animals, 10, 11
beaches, 6, 15
capital (see Guatemala City)
Caribbean Sea, 4
Central America, 4, 5
cities, 12
floods, 9
food, 16, 17
Guatemala City, 4, 5
Guatemala facts, 20–21
map, 5
mountains, 6, 10
music, 15
Pacific Ocean, 4
people, 12, 18, 19
Rab'in Ajaw, 19
rain forests, 6, 10

say hello, 13
seasons, 9
Semana Santa, 18
soccer, 14
Spanish, 12, 13
storms, 9
Tajumulco Volcano, 6, 7
weather, 8, 9

The images in this book are reproduced through the courtesy of: Aleksandar Todorovik, cover; Fredy Estuardo Maldonado, cover; Byron Ortiz, pp. 3, 4-5, 16 (corn); Galyna Andrushko, p. 6; Jairo Garrido, pp. 6-7; Leonid Andronov, pp. 8-9; kirstyokeeffe, p. 9; Ondrej Prosicky, pp. 10-11; reisegraf, p. 11 (Yucatán black howler monkey); PhotocechCZ, p. 11 (jaguar); Cezary Wojkowski, p. 11 (black iguana); COULANGES, p. 11 (leatherback sea turtle); Diego Grandi, p. 12; Kyle M Price, pp. 12-13, 14-15; Lucy.Brown, pp. 15, 18-19; SALMONNEGRO-STOCK, pp. 16 (*pepián*), 17; Fanfo, p. 16 (*tostadas*); Patricia Palacio Ortiz, p. 16 (spiced hot chocolate); titoOnz, p. 20 (flag); WENN Rights Ltd/ Alamy, p. 20 (Gaby Moreno); Maria Palacios, p. 21 (Lake Atitlán); Francisco Sandoval Guate, p. 21 (Tikal National Park); SL-Photography, p. 21 (Antigua); I Wayan Sumatika, p. 22.

24